The Fisherman's Whore

DAVE SMITH

The Fisherman's Whore

Ohio University Press: Athens

ACKNOWLEDGMENTS

The author and the publisher gratefully acknowledge permission to reprint the following poems which originally appeared in these magazines: "Chagall And I Prepare Our Colors," *American Scholar*; "The Orphaned Bear," *The Back Door*; "Parkersburg, W. Va.," *Commonweal*; "An Old Whore Speaks To A Young Poet," *Counter/Measures*; "The Dumb Earth," *Crazy Horse*; "The Fisherman's Whore," *Forum*; "Cannonball," *Foxfire*; "The Fisherman's Candy Store," *Florida Quarterly*; "Little Badger," *Illinois Quarterly;* "The Tattooed Man," *Kansas Quarterly*; "Notes From A Woman's War Record," *La Huerta*; "Head Feint, Forearm, And Glory," "The Powerless House," *The Little Magazine*; "Among the Oyster Boats At Plum Tree Cove" (originally published as "Going Back"), *Minnesota Review*; "The Ring," *Mississippi Review*; "Hard Times, But Carrying On," *Monmouth Review*; "One For Rod Steiger" (originally published as "Case In Plot"), *The Nation*; "The Lost Hunter In The Dismal Swamp," *Northwest Review*; "What Lady, He Said," *Ohio Review*; "A Letter To Mrs. Anderson On The Late Rape" (originally published as "The Letter"), *Open Places*; "The Fish On The Wall," "Fish Song At One, Two, Three," *Poem*; "The Reduction Of Winfield Townley Scott," "Lael's Song" (originally published as "Late Song For The Coming Child"), *Poetry Northwest*; "The Cat Asleep In Our Moon," *Poetry Venture*; "The Scop," *Shenandoah*; "Mending Crab Pots," *Small Pond*; "For Michael, Dead In The Flop House," *Southern Humanities Review*; "Rooster Smith's Last Log Canoe," *Southern Review*; "A Daylight Lady," *Southern Poetry Review*; "The Show At The Bijou," "Hammy's Boat Circling Through The Moon" (originally published as "The Boat Circling"), *Sou'wester*; "Poem For My Mother," *Sumac*; "The Lady Who Got Fixed" (originally published as "Getting Fixed"); *Westigan Review*; "The Shark In The Rafters," *Carleton Miscellany*.

Printed in the United States of America
by The Watkins Printing Company
Designed by Harold M. Stevens

ac ā hafap langunge   sē-pe on lagu fundap   *THE SEAFARER*

For
William Carmines
& for Dabney Stuart

CONTENTS

PART I

PART II

The Fisherman's Whore

PART I

THE FISHERMAN'S WHORE

Like gentle swells
of corn rows that will not fade
from golf course fairways
or lost burial mounds,
their small silhouettes

rise from the sweat,
from beaded black marsh mud where
the city's debris bleaches
to colors bright as
children's frosty breath.

Along the swing-laden
porches of whitewashed houses you
can hear the lacy swamp grass
rake angrily, bladed
now in winter's first wind.

Deeply rattling throats,
old fishermen sag back against caved-in
hulls of buried derelicts
grey as pauper's bones
scattered on the tide's whim.

Mother-of-pearl garlands
their flanks, scales, coiled sea worms,
smooth shells deck like jewels
the soft womanish skins
where blood-rust lavishly freckles

darker. Sighs well easily
from ash still green at close joints
of the ulcerous hulks too old
for bearing men safely
through the last sharp tides

3

of the unforgotten ways.
The children have seen this, waking
as in old dreams; they sail always
between the proud thighs
of their fathers' fabled whores.

Today another one goes,
bicycle stacked by a stinking creek,
to chip, to paint, to curse
his lover's pure sweat
as he conceives his own possible life.

FOR THE MAN IN THE CHESAPEAKE BAY

I continue to discuss you, my madness
a perversity of rehearsing
how the sea breathes.

You and I, my friend, are spineless
as jellyfish in summer,
in their Ophelia skirts

blooming to the top of the water,
only to fall when touched
because we believe

the tide is regular as old men.
Did I tell you that
in the water

you cannot be stung, that the first coming
in air is what does it,
the red wound?

NEAR THE DOCKS

There was a fire in the night;
across the street I slept among the others
as the warm ashes snowed into pines.
I slept owning nothing, a child ignorant
of the blisters of light.
But the man who owned two houses
was also fortunate, losing
neither the old one whose windows bagged
with weariness, nor the one half-built
whose roofless, green timbers
were shriving themselves all summer.

I woke and he was sitting at his stool
where I had found him each morning,
half way between the houses,
his hands weaving the wire to a trap,
making the awkward small jerks
a fish lives by. Beyond him, his wife
already had begun to stretch the skins
of her wash in first light, and a dog
lapped from the ruts of the fire trucks.
I saw how little had been changed by fire,
only the tool shed limp as a black dress
in a heap which left a new, tidy hole
in the landscape. And now I remember
seeing also, as if for the first time,
the slate grey hand of the sea, where
far off the figures of boats crossed,
wove, and sank as they burned in the sun.

AMONG THE OYSTER BOATS AT PLUM TREE COVE

I have been away growing old
at the heart of another country
where there are no boats crumbling,
or small crabs with scuttling tools.
These pines warped with early snow,
this light that slopes and breaks
as the sea slides and sloughs
against your air and earth-borne
flanks: I had loosed the dead
from memory but, coming back
confused, I find them waiting
here at the sea's rattling edge.

It is too much to speak to them, yet
to them through you I bow, politely
soiled and whiskered, wanting a drink,
to stand under the old harsh throats
sharing whiskey at Plum Tree, among
the booted ones with plaid shirts
and large loving hands. But wanting it
is not enough; you only groan or
roll and the village sleeps off
its wild hours among neat azealas.
I stand among you tasting silence
as the wind softly licks the wave.

THE SHARK IN THE RAFTERS

for Jim Applewhite

Under the stuttered snatch of the winch
they draw him by pulley and wheel.
Slower than the shadows of night
tracking the sun through warm furrows,
he rises into the open fishhouse
where the sea flicks its blue haze
through a hole in the slatted pier.

It is not this mechanical shriek, but another,
like that of a reed blown on in the palm,
which reaches the women and brings them
out of the darkness of pine needles
through the labyrinths of swampgrass
where ruptured boats lie half-buried.

Some come as widows and some as children,
but everyone comes as lover
to stand facing this last house at the point
where there are no windows, no doors,
only a roof and a mild iron-headed animal
who cannot swim or walk but is
at ease in air like a diving bird,

all possessed
by his long timber-shaking shadow,
whispering like women who know the quick mouths
in the sea are the reddest hearts, whispering
he is beautiful and terrible, terrible.

And this afternoon as they take
the steel bar to his unmerciful jaws,
freeing the stump of a man's leg, the fishermen
free also the old malice of soft faces
where rancid water burns and flows through a house
floor from a mouth hung in a wrenched smile,

8

and each of the women close at the ravelling edge
as if to reach out through water and air
one delicate finger along a forbidden hide,
blue and black a single gleam in the heat,
as he enters the space between the eyes
and the sun that is falling.

Even the children who pretend in the dead boats
they are bringing him in alone, tamed,
remember what they know of holes huge in the nets
and are still as the shadow halved
by the sun and the roof is cranked up
in the rafters where a young man waits
and fingers the promise of a knife.

Then one by one the teeth are pulled,
the eyes gouged, plopped in a paper bag,
the baby bones drawn whole and shining,
the flesh ripped away in tongue-like sheets,
the entrails and heart loosed, coiled,

until only the naked jaw remains,
the raw blush of mythical gums and chunks
of a fisherman's leg
all debris, gobbets bloodied and sparkling
as they fall through the housefloor
and drift toward the feet of the women,
the naked, hungry children, the unburied
boats as still as mutes; and a man
begins at last to descend among them.

And this afternoon
while her children plunge and dive in the light,
a woman shall climb stairs and lie
with only a swimmer's shadow
on her breast, in the room
where a clock's familiar rasp
makes her spin and whisper

as if to a face crusted with salt,
a mouth cracked like summer clouds, bearing
the white sheer teeth of the shark
that follows her everywhere.

TOO EARLY TO GO HOME, TOO LATE TO GO ANYWHERE

We caught him hitching in the headlights,
'Jeremiah, odd name',
stunned him like a lynx.
Drinking hard, driving nowhere
we were men in rubber boots that
flapped like broken bird wings.

He drank with us, young men unnamed,
a little wild, 'like I used to be',
and he said 'turn here' or 'there'
and once 'I knew a girl lived there'.
Under streetlights, his cheek grew hair
like reeds in moonlight, his eyes
glowed like oil lamps.

'You can let me out anywhere, I know all
the roads'. We sipped and followed his arm
through cars and houses that slept.
Somewhere under a light we turned, held,
watched him throw the rock up and seal
the darkness in like a closing door.

We drank, following the only lights in town
through glass shattered like promises,
circling with Jeremiah in the back seat,
phosphorescent as an old fish in a net,
inventing history and women, breaking lights,

wearing our fathers' boots,
outlaws on the backroads of the dreamers
where Jeremiah, odd name, pitched and waited
to drink anybody's, go anywhere.

ROOSTER SMITH'S LAST LOG CANOE

– at the Mariner's Museum

Suspended in a vast pendulum of blue light
they keep alive the legends of boats,
the whole evolution of their making

huddled beneath the giant bust
of an American Eagle
whose wings filter the sun, whose

talons press and hold a huge brass dial
which spreads time on the floor
like moss in a cove.

Each step drops a man deeper in the Eagle's
eye, and there is one room Rooster
lives in, a man recognizable

by the scars on his hand or the shy
shadowy way he poses by his last boat,
as if he is saying again and again

this one is for you, this I have well built.
His arm bends into the curved bow
and the chines of heartwood.

On that wall there is a series of photographs
as precise and stiff as half inch
sheets of James River ice.

In the first, a tree, fully leafed, rippled
sunshine on slack water in the rear.
Nothing else has happened.

Rooster stands then by the corpse of an ancient
trunk, his saw baring its teeth like a fish.
He seems sad or winded.

Two men, one shadowed and grim, one lighter, lean
into the hollowed body of wood, their faces
turned up, surprised. Here, the river ribbons flat.

A keel rises in the bladed reeds. Ribs glisten.
The men lean on each other; wood chips
fleck the grey earth like stars.

A mast leads the eye to the center of the river
where specks seem loose, errant, whipped
by wind's domination. No men appear.

On Model-A-Wheels, she strains at the edge
of Deep Creek Point. Pines like massive wings
hover over the hull. Rooster looks

to the next photograph where she is under way.
He is missing, and the other man.
It is marked THE LAST BAY CANOE.

Under the final frame, the green hull sleeps
in its chocks, a tree full of warm light,
its body groaning for water. Your hand,

which once swung from Rooster's calloused fingers,
presses the chines to feel where blade,
fire, sweat made their marks.

These things do not show in two-dimensional gloss.
Pain in the chest, arm-breaking knots,
northeast storms escape this room.

But with the hand speaking to the wood, under
the Eagle's time-splintering gaze,
a wind in a wind begins to blow.

You listen the way a child does, feeling
in the open chinks and caulkless seams
for Rooster's empty bottles.

Everything is exactly right, the dark stain
on the stern seat, the heavy chain links
played out, the bird circling overhead.

In that dusk-deflected light you are told
your grandmother's torn skirt still remains,
a piece of the sea's tongue in wood's belly.

HARD TIMES, BUT CARRYING ON

His eyes were once blue and pure
as the Bay, but that too
turned thick with grim
trails of tasteless oil and shapeless

carps of paper whose words, bleached,
seeped away on the slow flow.
He owns the same boat, boots,
and seine he started with forty winters

back, when running in and out alone was
possible blind drunk, on the nose.
He steers by a plain stick
and ropes; fancy wheels confuse him;

spits on the gilded engines that stutter
in bad weather, lacking control
even when all else is flush.
They ridicule the radar in his head,

the barometer in his bones, and shake
the air with sleek wakes. Even so,
he works his hole with craft,
eats fish for lunch at noon and dots

it with a single swallow of rye, then
drags back hard on the surging
net, while all around the bags
crank up slack as widow's dugs in rain.

CAPTAIN CARMINES' DEATH SONG

*. . . the vessal swamped, filled with water and settled on
the shoal, leaving only her single mast above the breakers.
But they were without distress signals, or life jackets . . .
clinging to the swaying mast in the darkness . . . .*
      "Anna May", THE GRAVEYARD OF THE ATLANTIC, David Stick

I

She cracked like a marsh hen's egg in the lightless morning
December 9, 1931: her gauges
needle-sheared, oil pressure zero, water boiling in
her manifolds, keel ruptured. We held her head to
while Hatteras Bight fell from her stern, and leeward saw
the world
slick, black as a meadow before battle, the moon hiding
its wronged woman-face as the heart
shaped boiler burst, sagged, left us drifting dead onto
Diamond Shoals.
We held on
when she began to wallow,
our faces and the sea's pimpled by ice
slewed through shrouds and lines wheezing like a church
on its knees; her ribs thrummed like tines
in a choirmaster's fist, mast ropes rang
with passion on that stout spire.
When we struck
we vomited
our cargo of fish filling the sea with the dead
odd glitter of stars   sand snowing over us.
We heard the anchor float with its chain at its cleat. Hatteras
rose in the hummocky grass shuddering with light,
the flames of stars and children,
golden-eyed angels waking
in the pine shacks where women rocked. Wood
smoke and flesh burned in our heads. Five

men with no hope
climbed up
forty feet of ice-skinned rigging
on a tree trying to root in
the sea floor
thick with gold, rum, the perfect bodies
cast away at the edge
of the New World.
We could see
we were creatures impaled: half bird, half fish.
We hung for three days
over Diamond Shoals.
Then, suddenly, two boats appeared near by . . . . The castaways
shouted . . . but even as they attempted to attract the
attention of the coast-guardsmen the mast swayed far over
to one side, dipped . . . and toppled into the chaotic surf.

II

Through a fog of black water
spraying white wings   they came   as I thought, the angels
of Death. In each arm papa held us, three grown men,
they came   our six legs scissoring for the Earth.
His body turned hard as wood,
we clung   as they came floating and spitting.   I saw, or
thought I saw the face of God. I saw my father's face
purple, terrified, a stone scored by wet hooves.
Breathing more water than air
he clutched at his sons, my brother and I, so
dead in their sockets, his eyes turned to the world's
darkness as if to an old time of bitter thorns, of
wind and the ghosts of fathers, sons
cold on the sleek sea-back.
William, I died
among the stinking fish, but lived cast-up
on the dreamed sand where grass is a lie for
cradling the weak. I
learned to live in hot houses
among the clicking needles

17

of women. I let them plant me in soft beds under the shadowed
news of the world.
Then one night you came, found
me drying out, clay in the nets. We drank, we dreamed
of sealight and the flat scud of an old whore
languid in a cove of boats.
With the moon we shook
the current through weeds. I woke in a fine cunner
drunk with the madness of sailing, to
feel behind me the world snap all lines, fall away, drift
as I sang for the sea   not knowing why I was
a man three days hung
in the Graveyard
but possessed of everything   taking the chance   able to rise
to walk like a fish   glide   dance with the wind
the life that is longed for forever.

THE WIVES AT OLD POINT COMFORT

On the last day they wake, like knives,
all knees and ribs and teeth cutting
the fishermen free of the sheets
and the flies banging on the screens
where the summer is storming.

Each one pretends her eyes are closed
as she stares at the man she must remember
at this table, before the hated bacon,
the plate of bleeding, dazzled eggs.

In her belly she feels him rise, thinks
how his sandy hair is more breathable
than water, finer than the sand
water is always stealing in the coves.
She must remember to remember his hair.

In the darkness of that night
they rise with the fishermen and bear
to the boats a terrified, womanish odor,
women who must fall back through fields

where the leaves hiss with hot winds
and children practice the curses
a father leaves like a hand on a breast.
On the last day sorrow blisters her mouth

as she remembers loving him, turning back
at the black docks, the fish scales
everywhere, tiny jewels, egg chips
like pockets of sunlight on her legs,
transparencies she must remember always.

THE FISHERMAN'S CANDY STORE

Somebody's father hangs on the wall,
his mackinaw falling apart in the closet.
He will not come for it again; his wife

says they can go to hell before she
comes after it. She went to high school
with the lady that owns the place, even then

everybody knew what she was. Candy store
my ass. So when she sees the coat
pass by on the drunken young man's back

she bites her tongue and watches TV until
the last announcer comes. She asks him
can't she eat something, she is so hungry.

And like everybody else he nods his head
into the dark toward the candy store, so she
says candy store my ass, and tightens her belt.

HAMMY'S BOAT CIRCLING THROUGH THE MOON

This is the dream I have had
three nights in a row, the dream
of the eldest son.

Hammy's skin is slippery; it stinks and glitters.

He is drunk again, he cannot swim.
His boat, *The Beulah*, wears all
her forty-five skins of paint.
Each one is whiter than the last.

The bay is calm as a breathing toad,
its green blue swell slapping
somewhere upon a shore, a spray
of moss pulling seaward like hair.

The Beulah spins, its one-cycle
Lathrop tracking over the ripples grown
at its locked and canted rudder,
the ripples confusing the hair in his eyes.

I know he is in that bay, a dog-paddling drunk

with no fins, calling his boat back
like a dog who wants the old hand,
but I can never quite see him there, only

the dream where the boat slowly goes around,
circling, closing in like a dog,
cutting the moon into tiny pieces,
a plate of hot stars.

A DAYLIGHT LADY

In 1826 Miss Ann Saunders, becalmed on the ship of Captain
John Kendall, ate her fiancée, John Fryer . . . .
"Notes On Survival," Richard Frost

The world we looked for in the dark, sweet John,
    was never mine in the sun. I heard
      sparrows bald in the breast lift
a pitiful cry of praise in the cobbled streets
    where filthy pools of late rain
      knew their sudden coming

as I knew yours: the splash of sweating pleasure,
    then a sleek shadow darted up, loft
      spinning down slow as the crust
of a pie just pricked and bleeding. I put
    my head beneath the lice-quick
      wing of my shame. I lived

for the moment you should come again, gin clouds
    riffling your moustache, the small wind
      my breath made as I waited butting
the dark roof of my mouth as if another heart,

not mine, beat furiously in my naked breast. Still,
    in that place there was a world to hold
      the way the bird holds fiercely
to a song of light when in every cobbled ditch
    the mottled dung runs thicker.
      I saw my face every day

grow dull and thin in the sea's insidious eyes, not
    married yet, and the new world drifting
      like a blackened leaf while
you slept bone cold with a bird's dazed singing
    where the seed burned my thigh
      and flaked off like stone.

Love has nothing to do with this, John, everything
    the world calls love and closes off
        at last like a fading scream,
I tell you to forget. How would you otherwise?

Think of hands quick as a finch winking at the light
    outside the hayloft, a tart and salty
        tongue, men sweating at bellows.
Where are you in all this? A gilded hawk, you pump
    in circles as I pass, then shriek, seize
        and swell me with a dream

I feel as a scar knotting the lids of my eyes.
    A bat, I hung in my shy hunger then,
        letting the light soothe
the others I had dazzled like a silver bell,
    my toes up with a vixen's cunning.
        In the dark, one tooth

remembers the other's song. Captain Kendall's
    daughter and I played at cards
        on the hot stone of the sea.
When she went out, I held the knave flushed.

When it comes that hunger does not slip the mind
    like pain, dear John, it sticks close
        along the limbs, singing to
the last instant. I began by toasting your arms;
    your white breast I savored with
        a salad of eyes and ears.

The thighs I kept near the end for warmth, and
    your skull I gave to a woman I saw
        rise in the sea, for I never
was a selfish creature. In cold clear currents
    I have seen you smile in grass
        where white gulls feed.

Tomorrow I shall dance upon a stranger's shore
    with the black wind of my heart
        beating for John Fryer.
In a sigh of light, I shall lose my name. What

    you were to me none shall ever know: your penis,
        your testicles I removed in the room
            of the stars. Like sparrows,
    for days, they filled me with your sweet praise.
        It was the most delicious thing
            I have ever tasted.

Now I sit to watch the lovers go along the lanes
    where shadows sleep in shadows,
        small birds sailing deep
where once my eyes lived, a worm stirring within.
    And this is my lover's poem,
        And I am a Lady again.

THE POWERLESS HOUSE
for Gilbert Page

Out there in the marsh's soft middle, the dark part
cradles her house and I can find it
only by following the black wires that tremble
in the wind, powerless connections, dead

where something like a bomb or a Ford has ripped
open a sparkling wound that cuts off everyone
even to the last house where the young girl lies.

Her reddish hair cups her head like a pillow
and she is used to the gnats in it.
She does not bother to bare her neck now.
She is naked and has been for a long time,
and as lonely.

She holds her hand mirror and waits
for the lights to come on, but her fingers can see
in the night the small hole just between
the walls of her rib cage. She believes everyone
is lying to her and dreams what must happen

when she drifts up the long road
looking for a guardpost in Asia, a bus stop
in Virginia where you must meet her
when the power comes back. Oh Gilbert,

why don't you tell her this dark is the dark
inside the broken shoe, why the wind bores
through the slant of her body like a sniper's bullet,
why faces slide off her mirror in the house where
every switch is a dead nerve in a green body bag?

THE DUMB EARTH

It is a large room
which smells like an attic,
where mold eats at the deep blue
walls. There are frames hanging
where the grim faces anxiously,
but reticently, watch your progress.
There is probably an old bed
holding a woman with snow-white teeth
and a thick carpet of matted
leaves which hiss as you pace
around looking for the thing
which bears your name. These are
facts you know when you get in your car.
What you do not know is the color
of the house which keeps them,
the street number and neighborhood.
That is what you look for
staying up late at night, reading
the Esso map where all roads run off
into the infinite blue border.
When at last you go to bed, dream
of the color of cities, massive yellows,
rural greens. In one of them
a window will open and you will see
what you have been afraid of, what
is in the eyes of those faces: you,
naked, floating in a vast blue room.

THE LADY WHO GOT FIXED

Today I watched the cat
who does not even remember
there were kittens. Slowly
I began to dream again.

I was getting fixed. I saw
myself bloodlessly stitch
shut the old smile my flesh
insisted it must wear.

My breasts became raisins
as I slept in the sun;
I began to sweat, the fat
heat baking my heart.

I dreamed you touched me
and I did not care, did
not remember you, did not
remember getting fixed

or the cat who came
like a weight on my thighs,
or the black hand of dreams
stealing inside my dress.

MARCH STORM

For three days the wind blew northeast,
reeds huddled underwater, bent back and down,
like birds with their heads bowed
in a winged darkness. The tide
held, came on slowly, not impelled
by high slopes to churn and shear
through narrows, but a wall of lapping
grey light mounting the back steps, came in
unnoised, huddled among shoes
at the corners of closets,
licked out from under sofas and rockers
to sweep the rooms free of mice.

When the sun broke the fourth day's wake
the water retreated in silence,
the boats sank, settled
in the tops of the pines,
rudders flapping gently as dogs' tongues.
As if stunned like drunks in a noon light
we walked into the fields, crowded
under the boats, in their intimate shadows,
to lift up our arms and show proof
to the scarred wounds seen at last
where we had always felt them.
All around us delicate seagrass took root,
billowed, while one by one lean figures
darted off as if to escape
the closing net of the night.

Poquoson, Virginia: 1963

MENDING CRAB POTS

The boy had run all the way home
from school to tell the old man
about a book he'd found which put
the whole thing in a new light:
'The beautiful sea, grandfather,
in a poem you might have written,
out there always to be touched
or swum in, or worked, or just
looked at, the way you told me.'

The old man gave the wire trap
one extra twist, like a chicken's
neck, relit his dead cigar, said
he heard the slovenly bitch still
ranted around, couldn't be got
rid of, or lived with. He slit
the head from a blowfish, stuffed
it in the mouth of the pot, grinned.
'Them poets, goddam 'em, always
in school with their white hands.'

THE SPINNING WHEEL IN THE ATTIC

Not for beauty's sake, or art's, this wheel
 came round in his calloused palms,
  bent willows and oak,

formed for the work of spinning whole cloth,
 gatherer of scraps fine and coarse,
  a tool, a gentle yoke.

Long nights he labored in the ways of stars,
 his back bowed at a shaft of steel,
  hewing curves and spokes

from the supple wood in his bone-yellow fist.
 No consideration of death's awl, no
  fear of time's cat

claws gouging out the wood's fine-honed finish
 deceived him in all the things he did.
  He wore a plain brown hat.

I can see his whittle marks as thick as scars,
 rough as rocks in any river bed,
  where he fretted at

the grain's refusal to have his slightest idea.
 My finger drawn in tremulous dust
  shows his sweat fall,

revealing a woody heart in several secret places,
 the way a wire buried in a limb
  buckles a man's saw

so in the dusk he curses low past a woman's ear,
 then bends with numbed fingers to work
  as winds howl and yaw.

30

At window, meager as old dreams, she watches him,
thinking what she will weave, shawl,
sweater or coverlet

for the bed blank as a grave in a dark corner, her
eyes working the grey thread from
the field's gold blanket

through animal mouths, shearing it, the coiled skeins
pooled on a planked floor, even patterns
linked as a scheme of planets.

She has no illusions in this, only a moment's delight
in what she might make from her fear
and the cold. The wood,

bared, glistens light and dark in smooth grooves
where she drew together the strands
until the stems and buds

of earth's glut silenced her humming eloquence. I
think of him then touching the wheel,
remembering raw wood

he had turned whole, almost alive, in her hands
like a metaphor of all they knew,
spokes, singing tines,

sparking in the moonlight as some fabric meshed,
knowing the machine finally was useless
as mourning chimes,

knowing his art no more than the rain-worn heart
of a stone, cut hollow as a cup
on the grindstone of time.

THE BULLETS OF CAMDEN, NORTH CAROLINA

. . . the most fearful and best contested struggle
of the Burnside Expedition.
OFFICIAL RECORDS UNION & CONFEDERATE ARMIES

A deepening works within ancient pines,
    slowly rises the shadow soft shimmer,
  wind or something worse than wind,
all drawn close, as water draws to ice,

around the bark's wounds thickened, edged,
    time's scab now utterly hard, that coil
  unable to free itself, imbedded, eaten,
perfectly pure in the wood's green blood,

but not so the pine's swollen flank, tissue
    rippled and warped forever, so, cut,
  planed, the slender boards are blemished
by dark whorls like an onion's heart, warts

growing deeper and older on the fine steel,
    until even roots and their frail saplings
  distant from the trunk as grandsons know
the scar's mark like an ancient disease.

The tree I climbed as a child in Camden
    still stands, gnarled by its wounds,
  linking a wind-swept tribe that cannot be
cut down for kitchens or floors or anything.

NOTES FROM A WOMAN'S WAR RECORD: LATE 1864

Town

He is not a large man, but fulsome of beard. He swears
he abhors the sword at his waist, the gilt
scabbard clinking like spun glass
as he turns to greet the young widow. Madame, so good
to see you in these hard times.

He must have spoken softly as the neighbor he was once
before the felling of Shiloh wood, the wound
of her eyes slight but dark
as hair cracks in a dinner plate. Good for you perhaps,
George, she said, her pewter voice

flat, hard as fox's teeth. They walk, they smile, cups
fiery with iced cider. A band's brisk march
smothers the ping of pickets
in North Richmond as girls in old dresses spin like
tattered leaves in a wet light.

He coughs, stiffens at one whose face he has known, takes
her mother's arm under his blue sleeve,
pats it as one would tamp nails
in horses' hooves, turns aside to issue a prompt order,
cocks his ear to a cannon's boom.

Slowly her teeth appear in strained smile. She sees
his uniform is thick with mud, badly torn.
George, we are all going mad.
Your son, he is well? He nods. I have news of your
husband. Will you waltz?

Country

Too terrible to speak of it, this unimaginable anguish
stuns the old man. He cradles the woman
in one gray arm, stares at
the worn bridle in the other. A man's initials still
burn the stiff leather.

The smell of early plowing is on him, wild onions, honey
suckle from the rail fence, damp sweat.
His eyes are the color of
fieldstone. When he drinks from the cold well, muscle knots
his throat. He says nothing.

He draws the heat of her fever with his cold hands, lets her
sleep in the quilts. White Dogwood
snows the fields to the river
and grows in the smoke of his pipe. He believes he can hear
boots thump on his porch.

When he speaks there is a sound of ice breaking loose, that
lean scritch of wood scraping stone.
He is gone when she wakes. Now
she knows her future. She will bury them all and live long
enough to savor coldest winds.

And she must then have gone to tell him, set the dogs barking
where the barn glowed with its first wounds.
Her note speaks of his hands,
blistered by furious work, how they fell in the moonlight, two
lovers with fine, thin hair.

THE LOST HUNTER IN THE DISMAL SWAMP

Often I think I hear you thrashing under the wheel
of the cicadas and locusts, fighting the hard suck
of the swamp, battered pipe in your yellow teeth,

a net of scars on your cheeks gouged by unseen thorns.
I watch from my cropped field where peanuts urge slowly
toward the ancient trees, but darkness comes unchanged.

The swamp doesn't change and Washington's Ditch flows
as brown as Cherokee blood to Lake Drummond, though tourists
take home swatches of moss and small bears, hungry, go

through garbage the city dumps like lies. It is madness
to think you will ever emerge from this lost ocean, bone
knife in your hand, lean as a cottonmouth: the last man

to hunt the Great Swamp and live. But myths, muy hombre,
let us live with the gnats, mosquitos, translucent skins
of dead civilizations that doom us to the long hours

in cold light. I think of you in a pure corner of darkness
where the rank, webbed net of time is stayed by ancient
impenetrable cypress, your knife marks deep in wood, like

a language of survival. At any time they could find you,
huddled like a fawn in the clasp of deep roots, your skin
turned to the mottled colors of peat, your eyes mossed,

narrowed at the light where you surface. At dusk I hear
the swamp's festering songs, unchanged, waiting, while
Drummond glitters like a starry knife hollowing soft pine.

CANNONBALL

Running through town like that,
mouth wide open and hollering,
colorful and loud and flat out,

going somewhere we never saw,
he waves to us from the crossroads.
Then we go home and dream

those unbroken lights are teeth
of the small creatures clicking
in the wooden night about places

someone woke up in years ago, drunk,
with the red-haired woman who
was loved, but not enough to stay,

to not come back here and sit
rubbing these brittle thighs, talking
endlessly of trains and tall corn.

NOW WHEN THE YELLOW CORN

Now when the yellow corn falls
freely from the husks,
a hard, jewelled dust,

the land clots our fingernails,
mud clothes each hoof,
and the moon, a flood

of silver swords, shakes its mane
down to a silk of ice
upon every breastbone.

Unbelieving, the young man
claps his woman close, weaves
with a nail's thrust

through the tree's heart, a house
to hold the heavy night aloft;
a crown-like crust comes

sifting at the shuddering slats,
comes from the mountains' height
along each riverbank

where fish hold still near stones.
It is the shaking season
among the seeds.

Surprised, he will wake with husks
stealing the gold of sun
from her hair;

lovingly he will press the pale
from her cheeks until she glows
warm and lost in the dawn.

37

THE FISH ON THE WALL

Scraps of sketches hang
on precarious, tiny teeth
from every wall in this house.

Rich as an ocean of leaves
flooding early October,
the colors betray him,

his fantasy, his delicate fist
cannot catch the expanse
bearing down, harder,

where the thing he has seen
refuses his chosen form.
Each squibs and darts,

then stops to wait and see,
fixed with that fast expression
of the liar lied to at last.

In every possible pose
known to green and gold
a fish turns a wide eye

on its maker, and the maker turns
to a fish with an eye
unmade, imperfect, an image

which leapt once in a slow time
when the father gave his hand
and the sign of a faith.

THE SHOW AT THE BIJOU

It is a temple of brick
crumbling among the swamp weeds,
needing a facelift.
Nothing is on the marquee.
They come from the pine and black paper
tents, their faces loose, coming
because the tabernacle is the only place
they have to come to, or come back to.
They lean each to each, a congregation
of weeds rooted in the sea.
None laughs when God swarms
Sundays among the gnats and mosquitos
where the red foreheads bow
in the long shafts of dust,
becalmed in a windless ordination.
The others come Saturdays,
loins girded for a meeting of salvation's
fine heros, their salt-bleached jeans
humped with marbles and small swords,
each ready to roust through spars
for a wanton woman and a treasure
Errol Flynn catches again and again.
Sunday's crunch at the Deacon's heel
may be Saturday's popcorn, the first stone
cast against unrepentant villains who
also can go nowhere else. So Superman
descends from a neat hole in the roof
to seize the meek and the unshaven,
to lift them by their ravelled collars
above the altar as Lois leers in silence
and Jimmy marvels at the adoration,
the whistles, shouts, chants, stomping
feet, the Gang of the Apocrypha
stripped to their human briefs.
In the dark of the pews boys
dream of their sisters and it is not
the hand of God crawling the taut flesh

39

under the starched lace of the bronzed
daughter chewing her father's words,
fearing whatever happens
when women fail before the screen.
One who has heard her father say God
resides in this place on Sundays
for the comfort of men and women,
feels the words melt in her mouth
and thinks Jesus must be the one
for Saturdays, the shy One
pinching her budded nipples as she sinks
lower into the body shape of
fantasy. Already she has learned
the small, wiry moves of ecstacy,
dreams of her own flesh coming
to absolution, though she sits
as inscrutable as Susannah hoping
the cold hand will be gone
when the flashing lights fade
and the swamp rises like a blister,
sits licking her unpainted mouth,
aghast at the abandon of her wicked
sisters who swoon for the blood of Jesus
and Superman. She comes regularly,
Saturdays and Sundays to her seat
where the light reveals another man
beating hell out of his brother,
a thing she understands, as she waits
calmly with her nylon legs popping
with beads of anxious sweat, sits
erect as her father's simple wisdom
to conceive a secret Lois Lane smile
for the hero's trembling superlips.
Without seeing it, she changes in that temple
of silver-shadow images, falls forward
through scene after scene until she is one
on the altar crying for the sin-ridden
boys in the dark. Each year she forgets
Superman and the color of Lois Lane's eyes

as she sings of women whose thighs
never once have blazed in the back
of the only movie house in town, the virgins
in the high riggings and tall buildings.
And it is we who lie in damp sheets
she must curse with her passion,
we who replay the stale films
in which there has been no other princess
save her, the one who received once
with iced elegance the quick salute
of our small, maniacal swords;
we are the ones who dream of her
far back in the sweat cool days
when the good cape of the darkness
sent the tide and all hungers reeling.
On Saturdays, for her, we spend our children
in the shabby embrace of the Bijou, glad
to keep alive more than the legends
of a sweet harlot and her aging boys,
living ourselves in the flushed faces
spilled like tiny owls from the crease
of darkness where Clark Kent dies out
and Lois fights the gnats in her red hair.

Bull Island, Va. 1968

PART II

THE SCOP

*A sort of Anglo-Saxon court poet . . . . He has been called
a precursor of the modern POET LAUREATE.*
                    A HANDBOOK TO LITERATURE Thrall, Hibbard, Holman

He could get away with pants
Herrick would lay on a woman
as a silk of wind,
geometrically arranged, rainbows
wandering from pocket to pocket;
his shirts flamed
with icicles of silver thread,
his cap was a comical cone
or a waffle of wool
and he moaned or he whoofed
with whatever it said.
His slight hose slithered
on the whitest of skin;
it had to be washed nightly,
the fleas and mud sent back
to the grass whence they came.
He offended no one with this
zany appearance in the marketplace.
Even the grim soldiers grinned.

After all appearance isn't everything.
Still, there were rumors, intricate
plots by the city fathers, guffaws
where the bores baited bears.
He held on, a bard in the best
sense, as he dealt with the dunce
dressed in the grizzly of daws.
He delivered the news from each
seam he wore on his flesh,
news of wars, of death
in the snow-capped mountains,
of oceans crossed and lush lands

where the fishmongers hummed,
of one father who beat his son
to a bag of squishy seeds
and was hung in a plum tree,
the fresh tails of the court tarts,
who, having made it big in the city,
took off their lace like everybody.
When he came loping on his little ass,
birds copied him, men stopped chopping
between their legs, and they told lies.
One hundred maidens held back
so long in the beards of briars
along the simple creek
prepared a truth as sweet as
heartmeat. He played guitar, too,
laid down on the stage in the wood
the acts of the latest rage, and good
man that he was, hung God's grace
like a critic's chronicle
above the mantels where whittlers
spat through the space of teeth
and applauded distance. Still,
there were those rumors . . . , they
questioned him, all this love,
where could it lead to? In the back
red eyes glared, and he knew it.

Fat fish he enjoyed and the wives
dreaming dulcimers opened hands
with the hams of their dowry-
thighed daughters, and the crabs
clicked in the long halls. Still
his purple ink flowed in fine
verses, fiddlers felt the pulse,
and while the world went slowly
round, he cased the windows, chased
the widows, and kissed the priests.
Simply put, his message was moral.
Not to love him was incredible.

Yet there were those who slit
his name with a dark tongue,
one half to the highway-man, the other
in the dung-stained tunic slipped.
He slept like a snake in the snow,
carefully coiled, not too long,
up and gone at dawn.

In his tracks they furiously toiled
like a trance of shattered birds,
for his lies throbbed like a lance
and he made them up on the run.
Fleet-footed, he fell among Queens,
warmed to their laying-on of hands,
eulogized their lumps and stumps,
their nerve-splintering elegance.
Ah, that was his undoing.
Jewel after jewel he stole, until
his poems grew sore and thin as mange.
And no one knew but he. Publicized,
he received the honorary sack
of wine, the right to ring
his bells in all the palace halls
and (this may not be true) a small room
where he could rattle his black bones
warm with vintage jokes while
he heard the earth clutch at its ribs.

for Jack Matthews

THE REDUCTION OF WINFIELD TOWNLEY SCOTT

You were the cheapest,
less per word
than bird or clown,
though still cut down
straight to the anapests

by the brittle old lady,
at the top of the stairs
to the mezzanine,
whose vicious scissors
have their own ways

of coping with inflation.
She knows what that does
to pipes, pantries,
panties, porticoes,
and poets of sensational

skill but little sales.
Worn down and thin,
you cost but ninety-nine,
a severe bargain,
but more than SNAILS:

A PICTORIAL LIFE HISTORY,
which says, I suppose,
a good poet endures as well
as those who ooze
through life's glossy story.

THE DULCIMER

It straddles a woman's lap, weaving her
arms and legs, the integrity
of her whole flesh shaking
as her fingers blur
on the strings and make
the queer notes rise.

Owl screech, snake hiss, jew's harp
and river whistle blend
as the bone wood cries, then
pitches low to an eerie moan
as the heart cracks and warps
in the child whose voice is a tambourine.

Along the walls, the rock jaws break,
their eyes turned up for a bird.
But the child's heart beats
for the wind in the wind
and the woman plays the long notes tight,
her fingers and legs and long hair bright.

Underneath the shade that slips on the glass
the birds fly in and out. A child sings
A miner's my man, a miner's my man –
Her hair flies loose above steel bands
and she beats time, beats time, runs
the ragged story line

and all the boots beat down until
there is no more than this:
slender knuckles scrape a wall
and rap down on a dulcimer's breast.
All, all around in the feathering light,
the ease of wood's heart singing grief.

ONE FOR ROD STEIGER

Get out of town.
    Don't want to see you
        after sunset.

Pack your tricks by
    dark if you
        want to stay cool.

Always the same, some
    quick, mean dude
        digging in,

townsfolks lying down.
    Night, the loaded sheriff,
        wrapping things up.

BAD MAN'S LAMENT

(after Lee Marvin)

Up late tonight again,
    me and you, Lee. "I wonder why
      I go for skinny broads?"

Listening to you, I keep hearing
    things breaking loose in the dark,
      the small, mean, scaled, slime

skinned things; all timed, precise,
    except we who sweat it out, not
      knowing when that one sweet sound

is going to split us open like
    a gunshot, the slow crack of
      a broad's spine as you lean on

those skinny, oh man, long legs
    like a wishbone we never
      got the right action from.

WHAT LADY, HE SAID

Let the shy boys covet
frail birds and spin
of them sleet-skinned
women for neat sonnets.

I have seen fine feathers
gum and fall to tatters
when weather plummets.
Give me this other one
of plainest matter.

Let her calmly kiss
me to the stones.
I am mad and crazy
for a dull-eyed lady.

Give me the slow bitch
with large, brutal bones.

DOUBLING BACK WITH BOGART

Bogart, the small voice,
  soft as unplucked
    cotton still with seeds,

dead serious in the weeds
  with his baggy skin, cloth
    of breadline gabardine;

he rubs the rubes raw, or
  out, grabs by the neck
    the elegant broads who

always are. No matter, things
  is as they is. Morning comes
    with the same rooster crow.

Browning said this better,
  but late, dark, Bogey
    makes believers of us all.

PARKERSBURG, W. VA.

Along the river tin roofs
the color of blood
release little rivulets
of greasy smoke,

longjohns hang in the wind
like loose-jointed ghosts.
I can see the current
herringbone

against the blue slate rocks.
I am told my grandfather
used to come here.
I toss someone's whiskey bottle

to see it spread out like stars.
No one notices this.
I wonder if anyone remembers
the day he fell.

FOR MICHAEL, DEAD IN THE FLOP HOUSE

Grey as worn lips, their beds
are tiered and canted as if angered,
but it is only illusion.
They hunch in them
quiescent as sand
herringboned in shallow water.

What they have learned is beyond
anger, the shy touch of wood's
song in the cop's club,
the black loveliness
in yesterday's news in smoke.

They are wise in what a man may lose,
old suits bag about their bones,
every roof needs patching.
Michael, among these,
I single you out
to praise a fine flint eye,
a cheek stubbly with light.

No one else remembers the fire
you kept our hands to. Now
the country gets straightened out,
as you straightened out, then
fell, swallowed in the crease
of the bunk.
The dark is always a long stick.

My hands are burning, Michael,
while they make up the bed
and rearrange the holes that remain.
If you were in the park today
you would smile: constellations
of newspapers drift under benches,
the trees are humming and flushed.

HEAD FEINT, FOREARM, AND GLORY

We're dead this year. Nobody's coming back.
Shotgun Brown, Coach

1

August. The pig field next to the schoolyard
vomits its breath into the clutch
of bodies which also vomits,
getting rid of smoke, fear, whiskey,
and the face of a corpse in the blue Pacific.
The coach's head count is short. A tackle,
two halfbacks, a noseguard drag deep mouthfuls
in front of a drugstore where a willowy blonde
counts her change. Others who could not keep
their heads down doze endlessly in sunlit
fields: it is 1945.

2

Shotgun walks uphill from the invisible fifty
where my father is digging himself out
of a hole filled with blood and dust. He
rises when the coach speaks, stations himself
dead center on the enemy's goal and begins to bang
his foot into the hands of my dead uncle,
lifting shot after unerring shot, his eyes
then the same flawless scowl my mother hides
in a dresser drawer, his hair long and slick
as wet hay on a hillside. He is piston-crisp.

3

Shotgun is a man of few words, a Marine: you Smith,
get in at guard and show me what you are.
Some things never change. The vile smell
of pigs drifts over me as I chop back my feet
and stare for the core of my man's throat. We are
both dark as corpses with the sun that pools

between us and he will never see my forearm lick
through a flash of gunfire and photographers
like a battle-hardened star in Shotgun's eye,
slaughtering the enemy and a farmer's pig so
they will say: you are your father's son.

4

September. The pigs have died out and the cold
whips through the line like a fist. Father
we have made it, me with the legs of the heron
and eyes narrow with fear, you with your All-American
feints: I have practiced breaking a man's jaw
with your forearm shiver; my elbow aches to kill.
We will not die this year or any year though we may
lie down with the dead and cry for glory. It is 1960.

THE RING

What is it this curious debunker wants
    from a drowned sailor's last
        remains? He rocks by a waist-high
        radio which for years has
said nothing, stares into the vaulted beams
beyond a yellowed ceiling. Something

he thinks of crackles in his ear, causes
    him to rise and seek the dead heat
        of the attic. Look at him turn,
        slippered footsteps lightly
thudding on narrow stairs as he goes

toward the dark he has not thought of
    since the birth of his son; his pupils
        tighten like inverted binoculars,
        shadows slide in the window
playing over his blank receptive face. He
quietly glides through webbed dust-covered

shapes: a woman's portrait, a blue dress
    uniform, tennis racquets hung on nails
        beside hub caps, jars of nuts and bolts,
        a wall of sealed, mysterious trunks.
His hands find the chest of drawers swollen,

stiff as the lips of a corpse. You can tell
    there will be a skin peeling in this,
        a small blood-letting. With screw-
        driver, he wedges an opening,
curses softly in the dim aura, then snaps
on a gouged Zippo that burns like light

spilled colorful and creamy through stained
    windows. He discards a Holy Mother
        Cross, hefts, lets fall a Christopher
        and a bronze figure he won for
running. Then his finger slips into it,

the silver cool against his flesh, then
   off. The swirls of his skin fit into
      the blurred flight of an eagle, dumb
         as a schoolboy's motto, and hedge
at the last vestige of tape which could hold
a girl's finger. It fits now; he wears it.

How odd it feels, the smooth worn metal
   he rubs in the dark like a cipher, so
      flattened by so few years of use, pitted
         he thinks by the corrosive sea. 'My
father must have been a hellish hard man'
he remembers saying to his mother. His hand

reaches back into a pocket of Pacific moon-
   light, glints, writes an illegible
      letter and signs it Love, Daddy. Cut
         suddenly loose it drifts like a stray
bullet against cold bulkheads, plinks down
out of his sight and fades like a remembered

echo. Below, a woman's voice surges upward,
   washing over him like a frigid sea where
      children are falling from his arms. He
         snaps the Zippo to his face, then turns
to descend, backward as down a grey corridor

to a wardroom where the coffee will go cold
   in his stained mug. In his right hand smoke
      trickles toward a foam of stars; a ring
         glows like a throb of sea-borne moons.
He wonders what he will tell them, what news
he brings from the attic and ashen letters.

LITTLE BADGER
for Dee

Digging among the dead roots
my wife builds the nest
of our house,
stone by stone
blunting the cold wind.

Under the grim, black-faced
leaves peeled like a skin,
she seeks a potential
stem or tendril,
a delicate tissue to
hover around us.

What is the price of this
gentle inquiry, this
ordering of earth and stone?
Only a man who likes
an eyeful of flowers,
so bright, so vulnerable,
could ask this question.

Digging, it has never occurred
to her to ask
what happens when the earth
opens naked in the night.
It is enough she has
work to be done.

I watch her toil all day
toward an intimacy
of earth
saying at last,
build Little Badger.
Some things endure like
a promise. I swear this!

A LETTER TO MRS. ANDERSON ON THE LATE RAPE

Sister, it is morning and I am alone. I have been
all night trying to remember the worn coin
of your face, conceiving a man who loves you.
Now I watch him let the robe clot at your feet
as his greasy mechanic's hands slide under breasts
only he and I have ever seen naked and lived.
Many nights he waited in the blind side of your
garage, his breath fogging in the cold, and then
you came like a dancer to tug out the last light.
He gave you time to prepare yourself in shadows
and with deft skill, came wielding a slender tool
to open the tight sash you had never locked.

Strange, I cannot remember your eyes, those tears.
What color is your hair? One man knows these things.
All night I have watched him dreaming, his moves
meticulous as a priest's. He has even torn his name
from over his heart and there is a fresh blue bruise
on his shirt. His gloves are as soft as child's hair
but he will take them off when he finds your bed.
He believes the skin does not fingerprint. And now,
what will you do? Who will you cry for? Him, him.

Ah, my sister, do not be frightened. It is only
the fantasy of a man who wishes you well loved.
It began near midnight when I offered you a drink
and you were not here, though there was a wind
clawing the screen at my window. I remembered you
crying across the country as you tried to tell me
about a letter from a man whose face I have seen,
how it began "I've been meaning to write, thinking
of you a lot . . . ," how I remembered your red hair.

THE ORPHANED BEAR

Regard Death as the mainspring.
Louis Macneice

All during the white hours that drifted
in sheets over her,
there was a presence, a blurred, winded
thing she could not comprehend in her blood.
                              As a bird caged,
goes mad against the bars, rising in rage
to beat its frail breast against the vertical
spaces, falling and flying up again while
the cat sleeps in a cock-eyed ball,

she licked the cave-cold night, she lifted
that heavy muzzle, made the stones howl
for the darkness coiling the inner walls.
She lay on her bruising sides, she sifted
                              whatever it was she knew.
It did not threaten her, or it did so
only as the dizzying stars had, by absence,
and terrifying distance
when she rose to her full height and pawed
the vacant night. Her teeth bared,
                              she felt her claws clack
like skittering sparrows on the cave's flat bed
when the moment came.
Two of you fell out of her squeeze and slept.

What was it she understood in you, or mistook
for what she thought she knew,
as she had on that other night
when a pine sheathed in silver shook
skeins of ice down her back and his,
                              that time the forest
danced whole in a long sweet shiver? In two
days she rose and with her one cub reeled
off in a dimness of needles which clashed,
meshed, a fabric tighter than fog. You
curled on a rock, sealed out like a scar.

62

You were a word she said
once and left, untongued, slight-skinned,
brittle as ice where water flees in a black
feather. If I look at your perfect, random
bones the dull wound of her one lesson
freezes in my skull, near the back,

a madness, a covenant made in the dark
where wind breathes, blazes, dies out
of the fur of loving, fading hearts.

POEM FOR MY MOTHER

If a writer has to rob his mother, he will not hesitate;
the Ode on A Grecian Urn is worth any number of old ladies.
William Faulkner

So now you see why
I have locked you
in that dusty closet
among photographs.

What choice did I have?

I often think of you
gliding toward me
out of long grass
with your eyes glazed,

a kind of heroine
from an old movie,
whose resolute face
is this language:

My son is a thief;
what will I eat?

But in your hand
is my autographed
photograph which you
present to visitors.
That, too, I would have
stolen if only
you had let go.

What choice did you have?

There is no truth
in any of this
but this:

Old women, like sons,
burn up with need
and they must steal
what they can

while they can.

THE TATTOOED MAN

At this distance I can still strut
as I did then, a childish pigeon,
head cocked, beading eyes alert,

as he winks with each grandiose
gesture. My eyes widen as he opens
his mackinaw like a secret and nipples

read HOT and COLD. He teases me
with a rose rupturing in his pursed navel,
repeats the adventures of a lithe panther

padding in the narrow canyon
of his back. 'All things are true
as we will them,' he mutters

and explains again the histories
his body bears with each image. A child
understands the worlds a man's blood

may contain and today I am a child
as I think of him and wish to touch
the faucet opened on that same park bench

with the old dark laments. This wound
might have taken shape at sword point
off Madagascar, or under a cottonwood

in Dakota where the Sioux brothered him.
But the news says the murderer, a boy
of nineteen, out of work, an addict

with a sick wife and son, panicked,
surprised by a counter-attack, and plunged
the screw-driver in his heart. His wife

claims it cannot be true, that the boy
was with her all day, feeding her
and the child who cries in his sleep.

How could he confess she keeps asking,
and who is this nameless witness
who says his guilt is indisputable?

'All things are true as we will them.'
In city darkness I watch an old man
tense again for a final threat

and fantasy becomes a public fact.
At dinner my knife dices beets and runs
with the blood of his wounds, and I think

how the will is the truest lie for those
who still live in cold houses, nineteen
and not quite convicted, though charged.

ON HER SECOND WEDDING

When we were children
I hit you
in the belly

the softest part

I caught hell for that
they said it might ruin
you

I didn't understand

If he hits you
in the belly
it will not ruin you

live with it

I put my best words down
as a gift
for your second wedding

I remembered the times
you cried
the bastards

marry our women
then sleep with strangers
I might do this sometime

I can tell you silence
is a living language
but if you have roaches

learn to kill

A CAT ASLEEP IN OUR MOON

The cat asleep in our moon
hazed window unrolls and cocks
his ear against the furred night.

She has come again through dream
silver fields, along the thread
of an alley, to enter his breath

on the small wind at the window.
He rises, shakes, taps a blunt paw
on the glassy night, and waits.

In the pines, almost inaudible
she is honing her claws, calling
with a voice like a beaten brass,

the old whore smoking in the night.
He does not hurry when I let him out
to strut on the shadow's edge.

I listen but hear nothing for she
is keeping still in a warm ball
he will have to find and roll

to prove his dominion. I wait
for it to begin as the waking birds
fly out of the pines and the beast

turns beyond any word I could say
to that disorderly house in air,
stepping with easy shameless right.

THE OLD WHORE SPEAKS TO A YOUNG POET

This is the way we do it dear,
    from post office to pier.
First you learn the age's terminology,
    tone and proper vocables,
the time to speak, the time to leer,
    the weakness of constables,
and then how one applies technology.

The bottom is the last lesson of course,
    the one that fills your purse.
Now when you speak never name the act;
    don't curse or mumble,
don't get drunk, don't get sick, worse,
    don't pick tumbles
who can't pay a whole night's contract.

Be elegant, but plainly dress, paint lips,
    keep little breasts, walk hip.
Steel yourself to do what must be done,
    avoid the freaks and simple
minded bastards who have to be whipped
    into shape. Be quick, nimble
of wit, have a good ear, and work alone.

Remember the equipment, take care, study
    it, keep it hot and ready.
Don't waste time on the frothy loves
    of children or senile
aristocrats: practice working slow, steady,
    groom your own style.
Success will come as sure as the man above.

Finally, take notes, observe your colleagues,
    both the living and the grieved.
Keep always something back against the time
    you're called a symbol,
which means they mean you're overdue for relief.
    But fight back, gambol
while you can, then go with grace in your prime.

ALLEYS

I have never lived among alleys
but I have loved them
as other men love fields
or the irregular grain of weathered wood.

Driving through small towns, I find myself
making change, plugging in
nickels for a brief citizenship
where boys and bums huddle in the shadows.

There is so much to be said for alleys.
I am like a scholar reading bricks
with their intricate, initialed histories,
the cracks unseaming everything, the love letter
wedged in the grit, still readable.

There are people who live everywhere, with names
and lives more open from an alley (who worries
how the back of the house will look?)
and there is a dog you can coax
from a doorway.

It is in the smallest things you can discover
the secret of standing still, the grace
unrepentant of an alley weed, the letter
which waits to propose love again and again
to whoever comes, the dog sleeping

in an alley, barking softly, getting up to follow
a man on a plain hillside.

FISH SONG AT ONE, TWO, THREE

for Jeddie

A fine night snow falls, filling the jade pond
in a field where a cow sleeps on a wind.
I enter the restless weather of my son's room
and he is dreaming among changeless animal faces,
feeling a fish we caught feel itself grow
possessed and ravenous for his small hands.
For fear, I lie down and put myself near him,
like a hillside the light cannot climb, but the pond's
pull goes on shaking him, his feet slipping a bank
so he falls deeper and something swims in his heart.
I touch him like a father breathing into the drowned
and when he wakes there is snow in his eyes
and a fish biting his feet under the blankets.

In every child there is such a light and a dark
changing the hidden texture of fields so a pike,
frenzied on a hook, learns how to breathe snow
and to run under a tree past translucent cows
toward a room where a boy's dream or a girl's
drifts, flows, and hovers under many fins,
many hooves hanging like the accused and the dead.
For them I will become the fisherman, the hunter.

If in this life, child, I have been but a mouth
numbed by sleep, lapping all light, all dark
with the ease of fields and ponds changing shapes,
now in your arms, in my arms I begin to feel
a cloud of bones gather and flee in the night
like a pike walking the stars for a lost pond.
Dream as wild as you can for I am like the trees,
a tall, shaggy roarer deflecting whoever comes
in light where the fierce ones do not sleep
but ride in the thump of your heart, and in mine,
a father with three years of roots in silver mornings.

TWO LOVE SONGS FOR TWO PAINTED LADIES

1. Chagall And I Prepare Our Colors

This Russian peasant, a man I know
only by cryptic things she says
when night has settled in its ditch
and her belly distends so sheets jump,
makes me jumpy, keeps me from the sag
of sleep. I can't quit thinking and
I can't think straight. Drive fast,
no wrong turns, dead ends, his colors,
wow, so brilliant, tank is full of gas,
his clowns have such energy, the moon,
why is it always tugging at the eyes?
She says they'll call everyone in time.

Yesterday I came upon her blooming gold
in the room where Chagall faced the sun
of late afternoon, the angles and sad
tanglings of a clown seizing her, fusion
of his art, her rapture, a sizzling silence
I could not enter, like a prayer room.
He looks, I said, in those blues and greens
like something nailed together, a figure
not quite human, but human enough to hang
in a child's room. For Christ's sake don't
cry, I said, remembering maternal blues.

Below the window an elm limb jumped, held
a bird with a straw, then flipped him in air.
Did you see that, she moaned? Chagall's
clowns make me feel like a bird. I asked
if everything was ready, asked again. It is
as if we had lost the old language, new
words keep piling up between us and I break
into open rooms like a bird in a wrong place.
If I knew where you lived, Russian, I'd call
to say bring the straw in, you must come now,
alert your neighborhood of angels and clowns.
I'd say there is going to be a birth, get
a pallette: you have rights like anyone.

73

2. Lael's Song

Child, often I am thinking of you
as the nights of winter
grow ghostly in my brain,
and in them I hear the soft chuff

of boxcars bumping toward a town
whose waiting lights
not even ghosts could cause
to flicker. And when you kick

my backbone shudders in its sleep,
wakes, often thinking it is time
to unbolt the houses we live in,
you in the glow of a long night

and I in a bed that will not rest;
thinking also how in one of those cars
there is an angel to introduce us
if, in the dark, we should forget

the things we have waited so long
to say. It is an angel of desolation
with the pale face of your brother,
its grief hoary but soon to end

as our hearts soar at your coming.
Keep kicking for it is time to say
the edge of the plain breaks, cars
begin to thud toward the first light,

and as the shrouding shadows cramp,
already there is a mothering wind
unhooding like an angel in a room,
and a father dropping doorkeys

in the unimaginable dawn, a man
who rubs his eyes and grins as
steam breaks through a stationhouse
and all creation steps down safe.